Ava Buttons was extremely neat. She organized her packed pets by height and shade and also organized her clothes as well as hair ribbons consistently in very carefully labeled drawers. Even at mealtime, Ava's plate was specific. She aligned her peas and also carrots as well as munched corn on the cob one row at once. While other mommies had to chew out their youngsters to tidy up their spaces, Ava's mom would certainly stand speechless in the doorway of her little girl's flawlessly cool bed room.

It was December 1, the date on which Ava created her "Dear Santa" letter every year. Her little brother, Bobby, had no collection timetable, however he was unpleasant with just about everything.

After finishing her research, Ava got the stack of catalogues she had hidden in the family room, behind her dad's favorite blue-and- green plaid chair. She had actually noted them making use of a rainbow of tinted sticky tabs: purple for princess things, red for ride-on playthings, pink for problems, and so forth.

The moment had involved pick. What did she truly desire for Christmas: the red scooter with the intense red cherries polka-dotted on its headgear, the butterfly challenge with hundreds of pieces, or the scientific research kit with great deals of enjoyable experiments?

It was well previous going to bed by the time Ava completed her letter. Positive, she threw a handful of radiance right into the envelope and secured it securely. The address read:

Santa
1225 Reindeer Lane, North Post H0H0H0

Rest came swiftly that night. In her desire, Ava walked through a woodland with rows of evergreen embellished perfectly with red-and-white candy canes. She dealt with the sky with her mouth large open, attempting to capture snows on her tongue. Each had its very own stunning pattern, dancing airborne prior to melting in her mouth. They tasted like pepper mint. Ava grinned; wintertime was her favorite season: snowmen, sledding, and, naturally, Xmas!

One week later, precisely 7 days, Ava discovered something horrible in her mail box. Amongst the costs, the magazines, and also the various spam, she saw something familiar.

" It can not be," she assumed, feeling her eyes go fuzzy with rips. Oh, however it was-- her "Beloved Santa" letter! She swiftly turned the envelope over to see to it, yet checking it two times just verified what she currently knew.

The envelope felt heavy as well as moist, as if it had actually been being in a puddle. Ava stood still, trying to blink away her rips, and that's when she discovered it. A note in little letters on the bottom edge of the envelope read: "Return to Sender. Explanation to Follow Quickly."

And so it started, in residences in communities, cities, as well as countries around the world. "Beloved Santa" letters had actually been stamped with the words "Go back to Sender," each guaranteeing a description quickly.

That afternoon, phones, e-mails, as well as texts did not stop ringing, pinging, as well as buzzing, as mystified parents discussed their kids's returned "Precious Santa" letters and also the meaning behind the weird little note printed under corner.

Nobody had a solution, however almost everybody had a question or two. Why had the letters been returned? Why were all of the envelopes damp as well as hefty? Were the letters returned only to mischievous children or to wonderful ones as

well? Was this the work of a disgruntled fairy? It wouldn't be long before all of these concerns and more would be answered.

The following few days passed extremely slowly. Time ticked by customarily, yet in some way, each minute appeared to take a lot longer than typical to pave the way to the next, as well as the hours were similarly uncoopcrative.

Ava asked for the 3,875,693 rd time. The very same inquiry was asked in residences all over, as well as, many of the time, it was asked also extra than 3,875,693 times!

Ava's mother had vacuumed the same spot of carpeting over and over, a lot of times that there wasn't much rug left. It had actually gone hairless! Across the street, Sebastian's daddy had not only shoveled the snow off his own driveway, but he had proceeded shoveling up until he would certainly cleared almost every driveway in town!

Waiting had been no less complicated for kids. Ivy tinted in her coloring publication till the only thing left of her crayon was its paper wrapper. Luke had actually been soaking in the bathtub so long that every part of him had actually come to be wrinkly, and also the as soon as cozy sparkling water was not only cool yet a funny color of gray!

Ava puttered around in her bed room, attempting to sidetrack herself by figuring out her sock cabinet. Organizing constantly made her feeling better. The

yellow set entered the area marked "Y," while she threw the flowered pair in area "F." She paused a minute when she came across the pair with apes and red stripes, trying to decide whether they belonged under "A" for pets, "M" for monkeys, or "S" for stripes. She would certainly come back to them later on, she thought.

Just after that, Bobby burst right into her space.

" Can not you knock?" Ava barked, angling behind her bed to fetch a pair of fallen green socks.

" However it is essential, Ava," Bobby said breathlessly. "We have an additional letter from the North Post. It has to be 'quickly' currently!"

Ava's mom checked out the unusual red- and-white-striped envelope. The handwriting on the front was the same as that on the "Beloved Santa" letters, other than this letter was addressed to "Mommy, Papa, or anybody like a Mommy or a Papa," and also on the lower corner of this envelope there was an additional note.

Ava and also Bobby cried at the very same time. "What does it claim? once more, reaching the very limitation of their inquisitiveness. They had actually waited for "quickly," and now that it had arrived, they couldn't wait another 2nd.

Ava's mommy opened the envelope very carefully, launching from it the

wonderful scent of gingerbread. It smelled like Xmas! She pulled out a letter, a long letter. The more she drew, the longer it got. After a very long time, she had ultimately unfurled the long letter out of the envelope.

Ava and also Bobby traded looks, perplexed. It was evident that they would have no option however to wait a little bit a lot more, since this letter would take some time to read.

As their mom started reviewing the letter, her eyes expanded wide with concern. The little handwriting supplied huge news, and also none of it was great. The letter said:

Dear Mom and Dad, or Mom and Mom, or Dad and Dad, or Mom, or Dad or anyone who is like a Mom or a Dad:

As you may have noticed, we recently returned your child's "Dear Santa" letter. We are very, very **sorry**.

There has been a very, **bad**

storm at the North Pole, and as a result, Santa's workshop has been

very, **badly damaged. We need all available elf**

power to repair the damage and hope that we can be back in

operation by next Christmas.

Signed,

Very, very, very, very, very, very, very, very, very, very,   very, very,

very, very, very, very, very, very, very, very, very, very, very, very,

very, very, very, very, very, very, very, very, very, very, very, very,

very, very, very, very, very, very, very, very, very, very, very, very,

very, very, very, very, very, very, very, very, very, very, very, very,

very, very, very, very, very, very, very, very, very, very, very, very,

very, very, very, very, very, very, very, very, very, very, very, very,

truly yours,

Reppetto Elfman, Director
"Dear Santa" Letter Crisis Management Team

Ava's mommy stood holding the letter, surprised. She believed to read it again, however it was very, really, very, really-- oh, don't bother! The message was clear: no Christmas desires would be provided this year. She had actually never believed something feasible, but sadly it was.

Dinnertime was terribly quiet that night. Ava stared at her plate, mixing her pasta and meatballs right into a sloppy load. Bobby rested with his head hung reduced. Even his hair looked bent and unfortunate. Their papa attempted to applaud them up with a promise of gelato for dessert, yet nobody was interested. They were currently frozen inside.

That evening, while cleaning her teeth, Ava overheard her mother talking with a good friend on the phone. Her child had actually just obtained his "Precious Santa"

letter back, as well, and the description had coincided long as well as very depressing letter. Ava sneaked into bed and also came under a dreamless sleep.

The next day in institution, the returned letters from Santa were all any individual was speaking about.

" My dad is going to submit a problem with the North Post," revealed Brawler Meyers crossly. "It's not fair. Santa must make those elves work even more hrs to ensure that they can fix the workshop and make our toys. I wager a few of the fairies are just being lazy."

Becky Goodheart had a various sight. "Just how can you say that, Rowdy? You generally wrote the lengthiest 'Beloved Santa' letters of all, as well as your Christmas desires were constantly supplied, even though many times I believe you were bordering on mischievous as well as not really wonderful in any way!"

Rowdy huffed noisally as he stomped away. He understood he was being mischievous, however being nice didn't appear to be necessary. He could as well be EXTRA mischievous if he had not been obtaining any of his Christmas dreams.

It was a relief to everybody when the institution day ultimately ended.

That evening, after tucking Ava and also Bobby right into bed, their mommy worked out in to watch the news, anxious to discover whether anything would be stated about the Christmas dilemma.

" Ladies as well as gentlemen, this is a special news bulletin. Billionaire Arthur Stump has just revealed that he and also a special group of expert problem solvers from his business, Stump Inc., are heading to the North Pole to assess the damage at Santa's workshop."

Onscreen, Mr. Stump, worn his signature gold organization fit, swung as he as well as his team boarded a massive gold airplane with the words "Stump Inc., We Are Unstumpable!" stamped on the side in substantial letters.

The following early morning, every person in institution was talking about Mr. Stump, one of the globe's richest guys. Certainly, he can aid Santa restore the workshop, as well as Christmas would certainly be saved. When stressed faces were smiling again for the very first time since the situation had begun.

Brawler Meyers celebrated, while bouncing a basketball during physical education. "It resembles my Xmas dreams will be delivered customarily," he said smirking. The thought then occurred to him that perhaps he should begin being

a little much less mischievous.

Becky Goodheart tried her ideal to remain positive. "I hope you're right, Rowdy," she stated, fidgeting with her friendship bracelets, "however I don't believe being abundant can address every issue."

Wild rolled his eyes. "You wait and also see. By tonight, every one of this nonsense will be over." He considered the pages and pages of presents on his Xmas wish list and also couldn't wait for them to be his on Xmas morning. He tried his best to give Rebecca a nice smile, the kind you utilize when you are asked to claim, "Cheeeese.".

It was well previous bedtime by the time Ava finished her letter. Ava smiled; winter was her preferred time of year: snowmen, sledding, and also, of program, Christmas!

Ava's mother had vacuumed the exact same patch of carpet over and over, so lots of times that there had not been much rug left. Ava as well as Bobby cried at the very same time. Ava's mom stood holding the letter, shocked.

At the North Post, the situation was not confident. Mr. Stump as well as his group had been flying in circles for numerous hours, looking for the workshop. With all of the snow as well as ice, it had been a difficult task, until a person on his team identified shiny bells, hanging from the ideas of thousands of eco-friendly hats poking out of the snow. As they obtained better, they might additionally see nine sets of horns and a pale red glow.

" Look there! Those are elf hats," somebody yelled excitedly. "And also those antlers, they have to belong to Dasher, Dancer, Prancer,

Vixen, Comet, Cupid, Donner, Blitzen, as well as, certainly, Rudolph. I understood his nose was intense, but I really did not realize just how bright it is. You can still see it below every one of that snow!"

They made one more loop over the location and also saw a great deal of activity around what seemed a large cabin that was miles as well as miles long, with countless twists and turns. The roofing system on one side was completely sunken in.

" That need to be the workshop," wheezed Mr. Stump, "as well as the damage looks very bad, devastating!"

Fairies in pointed yellow building and construction hats were carrying out thousands of soggy toys, ruined by the storm. It was fantastic to see elf magic at job, since couple of people had ever before had the chance to witness it.

The elves functioned at lightning rate, there was plainly little opportunity that the work would certainly be finished in time for Christmas. In addition, if the fairies were working on repair work, they were not building toys. Mr. Stump as well as his group sat quietly over it all, moving in circles in their golden aircraft, thinking about feasible ways that they might help.

It was quite a long time prior to Mr. Stump stood and rubbed his hands together excitedly.

" I think I have an option!" His group rested secured.

"It is ordinary to see that the fairies require help. At Stump Inc., we have thousands of workers. I am particular that we can conserve Christmas."

The staff member applauded weakly, as if their hands had turned into rubber. It was an intriguing idea, but would it function? They were also timid to confess that, inside, they were uncertain.

" Please radio Santa and also allow him recognize that we would like to land," Mr.

Stump bought his pilot, using a gold microphone.

" Sorry, sir," the pilot replied. "There is no place to land. The snow is

What if we land on top of some of Santa's fairies? We have also obtained information that one more storm is on the way!

Mr. Stump scraped his head, careful not to ruin his perfectly combed, gold locks. He and also his team attempted as well as attempted to locate a place to land, yet the storm had actually covered the whole North Post in a really hefty covering of snow. With little gas and also another tornado en route, they had no other selection but to return to the gold headquarters of Stump Inc. They would not have the ability to bring employees to the North Pole. Provided the scenarios, the suggestion simply would not work.

That evening, Ava, Bobby, and also their moms and dads sat glued to the television. An upgrade had been assured to be broadcast online from the head office of Stump Inc.

A group of stylists was active making certain Mr. Stump looked excellent. He had a golden credibility, one that might not be stained.

Seated behind a huge gold desk, Mr. Stump talked. His team members were amazed, since when they had last seen Mr. Stump, he, also, was glum that they had actually not discovered an option to the problem.

" Hey there, everyone! We have simply returned from the North Post, and also we are depressing to report that the situation is worse than we would certainly envisioned. Santa's workshop has been nearly totally destroyed. Santa will certainly be joining us by satellite to ensure that we can discuss a possible service. Santa, are you there?" he asked noisally, encountering a big gold display.

" Ho, ho, ho, Mr. Stump, yes, I am below, and also I can hear you loud and also clear." Santa looked like his playful self, yet he appeared weak and tired.

" We were incapable to land at the North Post, Santa, so I hesitate we can not bring any type of Stump employees to assist repair your workshop."

" Yes, I know," Santa reacted.

"The snow is so deep that the fairies have actually developed tunnels to obtain from one location to another. The passages are elf sized, so bringing any individual here taller than a fairy would certainly not be a great idea. I can just about get an arm via several of the passages!"

The cam relocated down gradually as well as rested on a serious-looking fairy, standing with his arms crossed across his upper body. The idea of his hat barely reached the top of Santa's boots.

" This is Reppetto," Santa revealed, smiling at the elf standing close to him. "He's been hard at the office returning 'Precious Santa' letters to all children, both rowdy as well as nice, and sending out moms and dads the explanation of what has taken place." Although his white beard concealed his expression, Santa's voice couldn' t conceal his sorrow.

Reppetto spoke next in a squeaky voice. "Yes, I have actually been working very, very, extremely, very, really ...".

" Thanks, Reppetto," Santa cut off gently. "I assume we've all review your letter.".

Reppetto flushed deeply as well as dropped quiet.

Mr. Stump was doing his finest to hide a huge gold toothy smile. He took a deep breath and also readjusted his gold connection.

" I have an idea," he began confidently. "If we can't land an airplane to bring our workforce to assist-- even, that is, if we could have met the elevation requirements-- what if we brought the fairies here to Stump Inc.'s golden.

headquarters instead? We can use weather condition balloons that hover short, as well as, since the fairies are small, I make certain we can squeeze great deals of them right into baskets connected to each balloon.".

Reppetto looked extensively frustrated, but he continued to be limited lipped.

Mr. Stump prepared to disclose the following component of his strategy. He motioned to his aide, that stood beside something hidden under a silky gold sheet.

" My group has designed an elf-sized attire," he proceeded excitedly, retreating the sheet to reveal a little glittery garment adorned with the words Stump Fairy. "The elves can work in one of our numerous substantial storehouses, equipped with just the very best of the most effective. At Stump Inc., we measure up to our gold requirement.".

At the view of the uniform, Reppetto felt his sharp ears get very warm.

He was an elf, yes, but he was no Stump!

Mr. Stump clapped his hands together with his completing words. "As you understand, Santa, every situation has a positive side, however I believe this might have a gold one!" he claimed, winking.

He waited expectantly for Santa to react, unclear exactly how long he might maintain his smile from fading. He kept his finger awkwardly on a button concealed below his workdesk, waiting to press it to release the gold confetti he had actually conserved for simply such an event.

down. "I have actually conserved Xmas! I have, I have, I have!".

Santa waited patiently, due to the fact that he never ever suched as to disturb joy. Ultimately, he talked. "Mr. Stump, I have known you considering that you were a little child. You have always had concepts and also a heart of gold. Your 'Precious Santa' letters were amongst the most intriguing I have actually ever checked out. I remember the year you asked for 2 gold tricycles: one for you and also one for your friend. I admire your spirit of giving, in addition to your resolution to help, yet I'm afraid that your strategy will certainly not work. As you know, fairies are magical animals, and it is this magic that provides the capability to make millions and also millions of toys each year, to ensure that they can provide the Xmas dreams of every boy as well as girl.

Nevertheless, their magic works just as lengthy as they are below at the North Post. Otherwise, they would certainly never ever be able to go on vacation without being pestered to demonstrate their magic, or, even worse, they might be in danger of being abducted by people who want to abuse their special powers.".

Mr. Stump was without words, something that hardly ever happened. He checked out the camera, his gold teeth concealed behind let down lips. His voice seemed tiny when he talked. "What if we built a large hair clothes dryer to disappear the snow?".

It was a ridiculous idea-- also he understood that, yet he wished to try anyway.

He was hopeless to save Christmas, but deep down, he knew he was stumped! Perhaps someone else would think of a suggestion, someone.

unstumpable. Mr. Stump looked directly right into the electronic camera. "I can not visualize a year without Christmas. Definitely, there is a solution!".

Santa took a look at Mr. Stump with his cozy, type eyes. "Arthur, thanks for trying. The large hair dryer is an unique idea, however the only source of power here is love, collaboration, and the spirit of Xmas, none of which have an outlet in which to connect a hair clothes dryer. We all appreciate how much you care. It has actually heated our hearts throughout an extremely cold time. Reppetto as well as I need to return to function now. We have so much to do. See you following Xmas, everyone," Santa claimed, attempting his best to sound jolly.

With that said, the screen went empty.

The next day at school, the cafeteria was uncommonly quiet. Christmas had not been coming: it was specific now. Ava rested at a long table with her close friends, repositioning the mushroom slices on her pizza. There had to be something that might be done. She was sure of it.

" Perhaps we can generate an option," she claimed to her good friends brilliantly.

" What could we potentially do that the globe's richest male could not?" asked Brawler in a grumpy, snooty tone.

"He attempted every little thing, Ava. No Xmas desires.".

"It may assist cheer us up. Bring your 'Dear Santa' letters. If you have a sis or a brother, you can bring their letters, also.".

That Saturday, Ava's buddies squeezed themselves right into her neat room.

Bobby sat in the hallway outside Ava's room, holding his "Precious Santa" letter. Ava had actually asked him for it earlier that day, however he had only just remembered that he 'd hidden it in his pirate ship.

sign hung from the doorknob.

Bobby crawled along the floor. The space was peaceful-- also quiet for a space full of Ava's pals. He slid his letter under the door, before enriching as well as running downstairs to the family room.

" Okay, everybody," Ava said, attempting to sound encouraging, "allow's look at our 'Beloved Santa' letters." Getting organized felt great. Ava might feel her mood lifting.

" Allow's start with every one of the letters that belong to our little brothers as well as siblings. We can relocate on to ours," she stated, flexing down to choose up the letter that had actually appeared under her door.

The very first letter was from Ivy's little sibling, Holly. It read:.

Beloved Santa:.

My Xmas dream is for a speaking doll, with brown hair as well as brown eyes. I guarantee to love her and also take care of her. I will certainly leave you cookies and milk by our fireplace, since you might need a snack while you're making all of your shipments. Merry Xmas.

Love, Holly.

As Ava reviewed Holly's letter, she began to think. A huge smile bloomed across her face. She had actually once wanted the similar doll. Putting the letter down, she ran toward her plaything box.

" Jump off, every person, I require to look for something. "Here it is, under 'D' for doll, 'T' for talking, and also 'B' for brown hair!".

Ava held the doll firmly in her arms. Ava had actually not played with the doll for a lengthy time.

She had actually proceeded to various other type of playthings, like 3 - bracelet-making sets and dimensional problems.

Instantly, Ava understood what had to be done. She can make Holly's.

Christmas wish happen. This was the very doll Holly was longing for. She considered Jennie once again and can have vowed that Jennie was smiling back, just a little bit bigger.

" That's it!" Ava yelled, making everyone in the space dive.

In letter after letter, Ava and also her friends discovered that amongst them, somebody had obtained the toy wished for by another child. It lit up Ava's tidy bed room. They had actually all forgotten about their very own Xmas wishes, as they focused on making other kids' desires come true.

Outside in the hallway, Bobby was back. He pushed his ear versus Ava's room door. He heard cheers and also laughter. He questioned what his neat sis was up to.

Rowdy sat in his bedroom, bored. None of his friends had been around all week. He had stomped out of Ava's house shortly after hearing her ludicrous idea. The very suggestion of giving his toys away made him angry.

"These are my toys, and I'm not giving them up," he thought to himself, fuming. He looked around his room. Toys were strewn everywhere. He saw the end of his fire truck poking out from under his desk. Didn't Becky say that her brother Luke was wishing for a fire truck?

"That is not my problem," he thought, kicking over his trashcan and stepping on a half completed jigsaw puzzle. Reaching under his desk, he pulled out the battered fire truck. He remembered the Christmas morning when he had torn open the present. The "Undefeatable, Unbreakable Engine No. 19" said the label on the box. He remembered it clearly, because the very next day he had proved that the truck was defeatable and, in fact, breakable. He had spent nearly all day bashing it against a wall to prove it. He had done that to most of his toys, but what did it matter? He got new ones all of the time, an endless supply. Still, something about the fire truck made him feel blue. Did the dented fire truck actually look hurt?

"Nonsense!" Rowdy thought, throwing it against the wall. He

slammed the door as he left his room.

He went outside to ride his skateboard, his most prized possession.
Someone had to be outside for him to play with, and he didn't care who that
somebody was. Today he would be a lot less
choosy.
The neighborhood was quiet for a sunny Sunday, especially since it

was unusually warm. Where was everyone? Rowdy wondered. Usually,

there would be somebody playing outdoors, but today the backyards were

empty, and the playground was, too.

A block away, he spotted Felicity and Catherine, pulling a red wagon

filled with toys. He kicked his foot against the pavement to pick up speed.

"Hey, hey, wait up, guys!" he shouted. "Wait for me!"
Felicity and Catherine stopped. They hadn't seen Rowdy since he'd

stormed out of Ava's party.

"Do you want to go to the playground with me?" he asked.
"We're busy, Rowdy. We have lots of Christmas wishes to work on

and very little time."

Rowdy was shocked. Were they actually working on Ava's

ridiculous plan, giving away their toys to other kids? "What a waste of

time," he thought.

Rowdy turned the corner and headed to Ava's house. He had to

find out more. Ava's mother answered the door.

"Hi, Rowdy, do you have a delivery?" Ava's mother

asked. Rowdy was confused. What was she talking about?

"Ava's in her room; go ahead upstairs."
When Rowdy entered Ava's bedroom, he could hardly believe his eyes. There, piled from floor to ceiling, were stacks and stacks of toys. There were dolls, race cars, hockey sticks, princess dresses, magic sets, space ships, tea cups, building blocks, puzzles, video games, scooters, train sets, and much, much more—organized, of course, in tidy rows.

"Rowdy, is that you?" Ava called out in surprise, from behind a tall column of building blocks.

Rowdy held his breath. He could barely speak.
"What are you doing?" he muttered, astonished by the massive amount of toys in Ava's room. He kept spinning the wheels of his skateboard absentmindedly, as he stared at the toys.

"I'm a little busy right now, Rowdy. I have a few more 'Dear Santa letters' to match with Christmas wishes, so maybe we can talk some other time. This has been so much fun. Everyone has pitched in, and once we got going and other kids found out about what we were doing, they joined in, too. We've been working with kids from all over, so that no one's 'Dear Santa' letter is left out. Just think, Rowdy, there are rooms all over filled with toys, filled with Christmas wishes! It's going to be the best Christmas ever! Mr.

Stump was right, there was a solution, and we found it! He helped us with some of the crazier wishes, like a fuchsia stuffed parrot and a talking robot."

Rowdy didn't know what to say. As he looked around the room at all of the toys freely given by other children, in hopes of making someone else happy, he gradually began to understand. He had never thought about giving before, not seriously. He was accustomed to thinking about getting. The only time he had been asked to give, he hadn't done it. Now he knew why he'd felt so gloomy when he saw his battered fire truck. He was sure of it. Even if he had wanted to give, he didn't think he had anything that was givable. He hadn't really cared for anything he had received before. It didn't seem necessary, when there was always more *getting* to be *gotten*. Rowdy felt his eyes getting wet, but the wheels in his mind were spinning, just like the wheels on his skateboard. It came to him unexpectedly. Suddenly, he knew what he had to do, what he *wanted* to do. Maybe he could still help.

"Is it too late to help?" he asked in a quiet, "un-Rowdy" voice.
Ava peeked her head out from behind one of the piles. She was so shocked that she nearly toppled over a big stack of video games.

"It's never too late, Rowdy," she said with an affectionate smile.
"Is there anything left that you haven't been able to find?" he asked,

feeling hopeful, as his heart revved up with excitement.

Bobby startled him, jumping out from behind a coat rack filled with

superhero costumes.

"There is one thing left," he said, "but no one has been able to find it

in wish-worthy enough condition."

"What is it?" asked Rowdy.
Bobby's hand poked through the row of costumes. "Here's the letter.
Have a look."
The letter read:

Dear Santa,
My Christmas wish is for a super fast skateboard,

one that can jump up and down curbs and do

stunts.

If it can have bright orange wheels, that would be

pretty awesome. Happy Christmas to you, the elves,

the reindeers, and Mrs.

Claus. Love, Matt

Rowdy looked at his skateboard, its orange wheels still spinning freely. It was the fastest model ever, perfect for all kinds of stunts, and, unlike most of his other toys, he had taken loving care of it. He had kept the wheels polished and oiled and made sure to carefully wipe it clean after riding it. He loved it still, but somehow he felt something inside, wanting him to let it go. He didn't know the child who was wishing for it, but it sounded as if he was someone who could love the skateboard as much, if not more, than Rowdy did.

Ava and Bobby were rooted to the floor, awestruck, when Rowdy handed them his skateboard. They expected him to be bummed, but he was just the opposite. Rowdy was smiling, then giggling, and finally falling over laughing. It was contagious. Ava and Bobby started to laugh, too.

"We have one final thing to do," Ava announced. "Everyone is meeting here tomorrow morning."

"What for?" Rowdy asked.
"You'll see," Ava responded, giving him a big hug until his face turned beet red.

The next day, Ava met all of her friends in her family room. There was no space left in her bedroom.

"I've written Santa a letter, telling him he can make everyone's wishes come true this Christmas. I want all of you to sign it. We have to hurry! Mr. Stump is moving the toys we've collected to his headquarters. Santa and his reindeer can load up from there!"

Adam went first, followed by Albert, Alice, Ava, Becky, Bobby, Carlos, Carolyn, Catherine, and Charlene. Diego, Edward, Fabian, Felicity, and Grady signed in red, and then it was Holly, Ivy, Jimmy, Jon and Kat who signed next. Luke, Maddy, Miles, Nicholas, and Olivia signed in orange, while Rachel, Samantha, and Sebastian signed in blue. Naughty as always, Rowdy scribbled his name out of order, followed by Tamara, Thomas, Tyrese, Wesley, and Wynn. By the time Zara, Zelda, and Zyta signed the letter, they had gone through nearly three boxes of magic markers. It was the longest letter ever written! The room glowed with the spirit of Christmas, as they sprinkled in a handful of gold confetti, a gift from Mr. Stump, before sealing the envelope.

At that moment Rowdy spoke. "I love Christmas, guys! I really do. I used to think it was because I would get lots of presents, but now I get it. Christmas is about giving. I still love presents," he said with a mischievous grin, "but I never imagined how awesome it feels to give."

Somewhere, deep in the North Pole, a million elves cheered. They felt it. The Christmas spirit was alive and well. They knew that time was short, and they had to hurry. After all, Christmas was coming soon, and they had to get the reindeer ready.

"Wait just a minute," Reppetto called out. "A very, very, very, very…" The elves let out a collective groan. There was no time for this now.

Reppetto paused and continued, "A very Merry Christmas to all!" he squeaked, with a little wink and a smile.

" On Christmas Eve, just as he had done every year, Santa and his reindeer delivered Christmas wishes to all of the boys and girls of the world. *THE END…*"

Ava closed the book and kissed her grandchildren goodnight. It was their favorite Christmas story, one she read to them every Christmas Eve.

"Merry Christmas, Grandma," they said in sleepy voices.

"Merry Christmas, little ones," replied the unstumpable Ava Buttons,

as she placed the gold-covered book back on the shelf, under

"**S**" for story,
"**B**" for bedtime, and

"**C**" for Christmas.